JOINT CUSTODY

FIRST EDITION
Published in 2019

Author: Randolph W. Mack

Website: www.RWMack.com

ISBN: 978-1-7337299-0-1

Library of Congress Control Number: TXu2-105-136 | July 5, 2018

Category: Marriage / Dating / Relationships / Divorce / Child Custody

Library of Congress Cataloging-in-Publication Data

Editor: Barbara Joe (Amani Publishing LLC)

Proofreader: Kiera J. Northington (itsthewritestuff.com)

Photographer: Eric Bennett

Cover Designer: Barbara Upshaw-Mayers (Aura Graphics and Design)

Publishing Consultant & Formatting: Eli Blyden | EliTheBookGuy.com

Printed & Published in the United States of America

DEDICATION

To my mother: Mrs. Patricia L. Green

John 11:21 "Then, said Martha unto Jesus, Lord, if thou hadst been here, my brother had not died."

22 "But, I know that even now; whatsoever thou wilt ask of God, God will give it thee."

23 "Jesus saith unto her, thy brother shall rise again."

24 "Martha saith unto him, I know that He shall rise again in the resurrection at the last day."

25 "Jesus said unto her, 'I am the resurrection, and the life: he that believeth in me, though he were dead, yet shall he live.'"

26 "And whosoever liveth and believeth in me shall never die. Believest thou this?"

Because of you, Mom, yes, I do believe I will see you again despite being separated by dimensions and time. And through faith, we still have one love, one action, one God and one mind!

JOINT Custody

TABLE OF CONTENTS

JOINT Custody

JOINT CUSTODY

RANDOLPH W. MACK

JOINT Custody

INTRODUCTION:

This booklet can be used as a guide to assist you in understanding the process and procedures of family court involving the care and custody of children.

Enclosed are the various types of custody that can be pursued by either parent, reasons for pursuing different levels of custody, the reasons the courts may use to determine custody, as well as the benefits of certain types of custody.

Also included is my personal account and experiences in dealing with everything from family court to dependency court.

The purpose of this booklet is to simplify the terms used in family court, as well as minimize the conflicts that will result from the stress of the process itself.

JOINT Custody

CHAPTER 1

Petitioner Vs. Respondent

---◆---

The petitioner is the person filing the paperwork to open a case through the courts. Either parent can open a case as the petitioner. This means that even when one parent has custody of the child or children, the non-custodial parent can still open a case as a petitioner.

The respondent will be the person responding to the action filed by the petitioner. The respondent will be required to respond to the motions filed by the petitioner in a timely fashion. Failure to do so could result in the petitioner's requests being granted by default.

Being the petitioner and initiating a custody matter, does not give an advantage in regards to the disposition or outcome of the case.

The petitioner will have to state what type of custody is being pursued, the reason for doing so, and why the courts should rule in the petitioner's favor.

The respondent will have a chance to reply to any allegations made by the petitioner, as well as state reasons why the courts should rule in the respondent's favor.

Keep in mind that opening a case does not give either one advantage, and although one could be the petitioner, the respondent could have a more favorable outcome.

For example, the petitioner opens a case and states the type of custody being sought and why. But the respondent counters and shows to be more suitable to have custody of the child/children. The court will weigh the arguments and base its decision on the facts presented from both parties.

From my personal experience, I was the respondent in a child custody matter involving one of my sons; his mother had petitioned the court seeking primary custody. In her petition, she stated various reasons why the court should grant this. Her biggest argument was I was physically violent toward her, that I verbally abused her, and implied I did not have a stable home or lifestyle. I, however, was able to counter all of the allegations and prove her claims were baseless. And, as the respondent, I gave reasons why I was seeking custody and while doing so, I requested I be given *sole custody* of our son, rather than primary or joint custody.

I will address the various types of custody in this booklet, their meanings, and the reasons for pursuing different levels of care and custody.

At the end of our son's custody case, I was given sole custody, and the mother was subsequently ordered to have supervised visits by the court.

When involved in child custody matters, whether as the petitioner or respondent, you should stick to simply stating the reasons you feel you could best provide for the child's safety and wellbeing, as well as all facts to support those claims. Remember, the other party will have a chance to respond to any claims you make and have a chance to counter. Regardless of what's said by either party, the standard the court will use is what's in the best interest of the child. The court is not interested in people airing their dirty laundry in court or using the court as a forum to engage in personal battles.

My advice to anyone summoned to court as a respondent is to do just that—respond. Although the petitioner can be requesting a type of custody you may not want to contest, it's best to respond because there could also be issues of child support in their petition.

Child support payments are based on your income, existing obligations, and financial responsibilities; the amount set will be legal and binding. Once this is done, it can, and more than likely will result in the garnishment of your wages, forfeiture of income tax returns, liens placed on property, driver's license suspended, and even being placed in jail, if you don't comply with the court order. So, it's best to respond because if you don't, everything the petitioner requests will be granted by your default.

CHAPTER 2

Marriage Vs. Relationships

———◇———

Being married and dealing with family court can have benefits, as well as disparities. In family court, being married will not only involve the care and custody of the child/children, but it will also address issues of financial support, financial assets, and the dispersion of property. When seeking dissolution of a marriage where children are involved, the case will be resolved in family court, and there will still be the position of a petitioner and respondent. The benefits can be that all marital assets will be divided fairly, and depending on what state it is, it could be equal or half. While these things can become a focal point in a divorce, the purpose of this book is primarily targeting child custody.

The downside of not being married is the father has no rights under the law, until it is ordered by the court, based on paternity being established. This can be done by a paternity test or by both parties' consent that the child's father is not in question. At one time, from my personal experience of not being married to my son's mother while involved in a custody case, it seemed one-sided and in total favor of the mother's rights. Even though I was the petitioner in the case, under Florida law, the male does not have any legal rights to a child until the court recognizes him as the father. I found this out after I separated from Audrey, my son's mother. She moved out of my home, and moved in with some of her friends living in the same subdivision. At first, I convinced her to let our son, Shiloh, continue residing with me until she could get herself reestablished. This meant he would not be uprooted from the safety and security my home provided, and he would be able to continue attending school uninterrupted.

At the time, we had an understanding that Audrey could see Shiloh whenever she wanted and to come by and pick him up without any restrictions or reservations from me. During this same period, she was working as an adult entertainer. I had no knowledge she was living right around the corner from me, literally two blocks away. I discovered this by chance one day when I was walking my son to the local Walmart, which was within one-quarter mile of our home. I'd purchased my home before Walmart was built. It could be said that the store became a part of our community.

As we approached the last street leading to Walmart's entrance, my son noticed his mother coming out of one of the homes directly in front of us. I recognized the house as one that was frequently a gathering place for young adults openly using alcohol, among other drugs. The home was owned by a single mother, who drove trucks long distances for a living. This left her two teenaged sons with the run of the house. At the time we saw her, maybe six to eight people were standing out front. In times past, this probably would have never been seen in the suburbs. But, with acceptance and infusion of different cultures, things in the suburbs have become more acceptable. They have become more tolerant, if for no other reason, so they don't become targets of those they complain to or about. My son went toward her, and from that moment on, my battle began. It dawned on me this was the home she now lived in.

All of a sudden, it made sense. I was under the impression she was calling once she got close to my home, when she wanted to visit him. Now, this explained how she would get there so fast after letting me know she was on her way to pick him up for an hour or two. She would tell me she always got dropped off close to my home to respect my privacy. So when she would arrive on foot, it did not stand out to me. In my mind, I was thankful she was not bringing different people to my home in order for her to see him. On top of this, she would say she was just going to take him to McDonald's, which is located inside of the Walmart, or one of the various other restaurants within walking distance of my home.

At the time, I welcomed this because it gave me a break to relax. When Audrey moved out, I was responsible for all of Shiloh's care and security. I took him to school and picked him up, attended all of his teacher/parent meetings, assisted with homework, cooked at least five days a week for him, and took him out to eat on Wednesdays and Saturdays. I made sure he was bathed and read a bedtime story every night before being put to sleep on time. I washed, ironed, and folded his clothes and laid everything out at night for the next morning. Every Saturday, I took him swimming at a park, or somewhere to play like Chuck E. Cheese's. Most importantly, I gave him lots of hugs, kisses, and compliments on how he was a great son, special, loved very much, and a smart kid. While I'm doing all of this to keep him sheltered, I find out she's been taking him to a drug house.

At the time, Audrey was thirty-two. The two teenagers who lived there with their mother were eighteen and nineteen years old. I immediately asked, "Is this the home you're living in?"

She acknowledged by saying, "Yes, it is."

At precisely that moment, I saw her in a completely different light. It was the same moment when I realized she was strung out on drugs. Once Audrey confirmed she was living there, I said, "Well, I don't want to stop in front of that home with my son to talk to you." Mind you, this is the same community we lived in together for ten years. All of the residents knew us as a couple involved in our son's life. Those two brothers were eight and nine when we moved to that area. It felt like I got hit in the stomach with a baseball bat.

As I walked away, I said, "You can talk to our son when you visit him away from that house." I didn't want to do it then because it was obvious that drinking and drugs were being used openly in front of the home. Audrey insisted on taking him up to the home to pretend she was introducing him to the crowd gathered outside. First of all, they all knew my son even if it was only in passing; based on the amount of time we all lived so closely together. Another thing was I now understood what my son had been trying to tell me all along about where she had been taking him when she picked him up. He would always say when he came back that he went to his mommy's house. I would just tell him that it was cool. He was only three, so I thought he meant he had been out with her when he returned. I would ask him, "Where did you go and did you have fun?"

The more Audrey insisted on taking him up to the house, the more I insisted he did not need to meet them. I was not going to stand there and debate with her when it was clear she had been drinking. I decided to return to my home and drive my son to McDonald's to make sure I would not have to walk past them on the way back. It wasn't that I was afraid of the people at the home; I'm six feet, 200 pounds with eight percent body fat, so I'm imposing. Besides that, they were kids to me. She was the only adult there, at least age-wise.

When I got about three houses away, I heard someone yell out a racial slur. I started to confront the group. But, instantly, I thought about my son's safety and reasoned I would address it later. I was shocked at how she could be a part of someone using a racial slur while our son was with me. Although Shiloh didn't understand it, he certainly heard it. To be honest, it sounded like Audrey made the disparaging remark. With her being white, I still did not think she had it in her to go that route after being with her for almost ten years.

As an African American, it was offensive. But to hear it from her showed me I had been sleeping with an enemy for years. After returning home and getting my son to bed, I was able to reflect on the events that transpired earlier. As soon as I thought, *I will deal with this tomorrow after I've had a chance to speak to my attorney*; there was a knock at my door. I looked out the casement window to see there were a few sheriffs outside. I noticed Audrey was standing at the end of my driveway with one of them. I opened the door, and the imposing officer said, "Sir, your son's mother called in and stated she was forced out of the home and you refused to let her take or see her son."

I explained, "I'm sorry, Officer. But she moved out over two months ago, and it was her choice, not by force. She's been stopping by once or twice a week to pick him up to spend a couple of hours at a time with him."

"Where is the child right now?"

"He's asleep."

"Can I see him? I need to make sure he's safe."

I agreed, thinking this would resolve whatever issue had caused them to come to my home. Instead, he asked,

"Do you have any type of legal papers stating the child's mother and you are married?" This would have given me just as much right to my son as his mother. Without a court order in place, she could not try to take him without my consent.

I replied, "Officer, we're not married."

"Do you have any documents from a court of law to verify that you're the father, or acknowledging you as his father and granting you parental rights with visitations?"

I responded, "No, sir."

He advised me, "Under Florida law, the child's mother has all rights to him, and until you petition the court to establish that you're his father, she can have him taken from you even if she has abandoned him for weeks, months, or years." He continued, "All the mother has to say is you are not the child's father, and unless you have something from a court, the mother can take the child even if she is homeless and on drugs."

After hearing all this, I asked, "Officer, what are you getting at?"

Then he said, "By law, I have to give the child to his mother. You can go to the courthouse later to file the necessary paperwork to be legally recognized as his father."

I tried to persuade the officer to let my son stay by saying, "I will go to the courthouse in the morning. The home she's living in is a hangout spot."

He stated, "All of the officers in my branch know about the home from the numerous calls and complaints to and from the place."

I informed him, "She works as a dancer from nine p.m. until three a.m., and if she takes my son, he will be left in the care of people drinking and doing drugs." I also said, "It's obvious she's been drinking heavily."

He replied, "It's not against the law for her to drink as long as she does not cause a disturbance or drive."

"Officer, can you please to speak to her? Tell her my son is asleep and has to be in school in the morning, so could she pick him up from school or my home tomorrow?"

I was hoping Audrey would agree, thereby giving me time the next morning to reach my attorney, Mr. Escobar, as well as the courts. The officer tried to get Audrey to go along with my suggestion for the sake of our son not having to be awakened and taken to a house full of strangers. But, fueled by alcohol and drugs, she was more focused on hurting me than helping our son.

Eventually, the officer said, "I sympathize with you, but you need to give the child to her while I'm present."

Although I was filled with what could only be described as pure rage, I packed up a few outfits for him, including school clothes, night clothes, and a few pairs of shoes. I also packed a bag with drinks and snacks for him. Lastly, I woke him up and said, "Son, you're going to spend the night with your mom; I will pick you up from school tomorrow."

I contacted Mr. Escobar, who coincidentally is one of my best friends. He confirmed what the officer stated was true, and although I was upset, I made the right decision to give my son to them. He advised me to meet him at the courthouse first thing the next morning, and we would develop our strategy from there.

The next morning, I met with Mr. Escobar and opened a case as the petitioner. After going from room to room, for what seemed like hours, I finally landed in the right office to have my case presented to a judge. Once the process was completed, I was told it could take weeks before our case was heard. I asked why it would take so long. Then I was told about the procedures that had to be followed before the case could be heard, such as the mother/respondent having to be served a copy of my petition, to which she had up to thirty days to respond.

When I heard this, I became despondent and could not accept this as all I could do to get my son back. By this time, Mr. Escobar had left to be in court with one of his clients. I turned my energy back to a nice lady I met at the Clerk of the Court's Office, while filing some of the papers I had to have notarized. I explained what happened the night before and how I felt my son could be exposed to danger where he was living. She said, "There's only one thing that could speed up the process from weeks to days."

I asked, "What's that?"

"You could go file a restraining order and include your son as someone besides yourself that she has to stay away from."

Upon hearing this, I headed straight for that office and told the clerk I wanted to file a restraining order against Audrey for my son and me. Again, I called Mr. Escobar to see if he could advise me about how I should include my son. He responded, "You can either do it as what's called a *friend of the court* on behalf of your son, or based on the racial epithet and the potential for violence posed from her and the people frequently visiting the home where they are living." I decided to file it for Shiloh and me.

When I finished the required paperwork, I was interviewed and given a chance to state what had transpired. I was given a temporary injunction, which included Shiloh along with me, restricting Audrey from coming within 500 feet of either of us. A court date was set for that same week, and both parents would have to attend. This would help expedite the petition I filed in family court. I was told to show a copy of the injunction to the sheriff, which stated I had been granted temporary custody of my son and would be sufficient to have my son returned to me.

As soon as I got home, I called the sheriff's office. Two came to my house and I showed them the restraining order to pick up my son. I told them about the house my son was at. I knew he was there because his school notified me that his mother had picked him up.

A sheriff said, "You can follow me to the other home, and I'll retrieve your son for you." One of them was the same officer from the night before. As we were leaving, he added, "I commend you for being resilient on getting your son back."

When I saw my son being escorted out of the house, we locked eyes. He ran over to me; I picked him up and said, "I told you I was going to pick you up after school."

At first, Audrey refused to give Shiloh to me and came close to being arrested for the interference of a child custody order. She was given a copy of the order, advising her of the pending court date. We were both present at the hearing to see if the restraining order would be extended or ended. Before the hearing, I had gone to the Sheriff's Department Headquarters and gotten a call log showing the sheriff had been called on or from the same home over seventy-five times throughout a few years.

I told the judge about Audrey's work schedule, meaning Shiloh would be left in that home with strangers, and how both of the brothers living there had extensive arrest records. I accused her of being on drugs; I used the sheriff's report filed on the day my son was returned to me, where it stated she appeared to have been drinking alcohol. I asked the judge to request she be given a drug screen to prove to the court she was not using drugs, before he considered changing the temporary injunction. He ordered her to submit to one and she refused. I told him about the petition I had filed in family court for custody and had a copy given to her. Then, the judge ordered her to respond to the petition while she was at the courthouse, so the case could be heard by a family court judge as soon as possible.

He decided to let my son remain with me until the family court received our case. This was based on Audrey's work schedule, her inability to tell the judge who would be watching Shiloh while she was working, her refusal to take a drug screen, and the number of calls and complaints to and from the home she lived in. Most importantly, she acknowledged I was his father. Because of the restraining order, our case was put on the docket for the next week. The judge stated that care and custody could be established then and there.

CHAPTER 3

Mediation

———◆———

G etting the restraining order worked as far as getting our case heard in family court sooner. The family court judge ordered us to go to mediation to try to resolve the issues of visitation, financial support, and who would have primary custody of our son.

The court is in favor of parents trying to resolve conflicts, rather than it having to make decisions for them. This is why mediation is ordered in all family court cases involving children.

On the day we were ordered to go, I showed up only to learn Audrey had told the mediator she did not want to be in the same room with me, out of fear that I would try to harm her. My response to the mediator was, "Do you have the right case?" I asked this because we had been sitting in the lobby filling out paperwork, no more than ten feet apart, and not one word was exchanged between us except when she came in. I asked, "What's up?"

Ms. Johnson, the mediator, said, "I'm aware that you have a restraining order against Ms. Beck, so that requires you to be interviewed separately, regardless if she has made the statement or not."

I said, "Okay, by whatever means. I just want to get some type of resolution, and I'm willing to compromise with her to do so."

Ms. Johnson asked, "What do you want to propose to Ms. Beck to start the negotiations?"

I stated I wanted his primary residence to be with me and Audrey could have open visits with him. But, on school days, he had to be returned to me in time for dinner, bathing, and bed unless she had taken him somewhere to eat before returning him. Even then, she needed to have him back in time for a bath and his bedtime. On the weekends, she could get him after school on Fridays up until 8:00 p.m. I specified this time because he was only three and still needed to be in bed by a certain time. Besides that, as I mentioned, she was an adult entertainer and always worked on the weekends.

From my experience with Audrey, I knew she would go to work no later than 9:00 p.m. and stay up until 4:00 a.m.

on weekends. I said the same rules would apply to Saturdays. She could pick him up whenever she wanted as long as she returned him by 8:00 p.m. Sundays, I took my son to church and cooked lunch for him after returning home. So if she got him then, it would be good for Shiloh and me if she did after 3:00 p.m. and returned him by 7:00 p.m. so he could eat dinner, get bathed, and be in bed on time. I requested she not have my son in the home where she was living because there was open drug use and more going on over there. The home was considered to be a drug house by our entire community. And lastly, I requested she not use drugs while she had him and not drink alcohol excessively.

Ms. Johnson wrote down all of my requests, and asked, "Are you finished?"

I responded, "Yes. I want to see what her response is before I address any finances."

"Okay, that sounds fair. I'll take what you requested to Ms. Beck to see if she agrees to your terms."

After about twenty minutes, Ms. Johnson returned, sat down facing me, and said, "She agreed to the weekday times, but she wants to be able to let him visit her at the home she's living in. She wants him to spend the night with her on Sundays, and she will be responsible for getting him to school on Monday mornings. What do you think about that and why?"

I proceeded to explain the problems with the house Audrey was living in and had the sheriff's reports to support my claims. I pointed out I was doing so because numerous calls were made on the home on Sundays. This was the night parties were being held at the home every weekend. I also stated there were only three bedrooms in the home, but up to eight people were living there. With the mother having one bedroom and the two brothers occupying the other two, there was no place suitable for my son to sleep. And, through my own investigation, I learned my son's mother actually slept on a couch. I heard this from a person who frequented the house. This same person informed me that she had let Audrey spend the night with one of her stripper friends. Audrey said she had nowhere else to go, so the friend let her stay a few days that turned into a few weeks. But the friend asked Audrey to leave because after working all night, she slept all day.

I flatly added, "As a responsible parent, I will not consent to my son being in a known drug house. It could get raided at any time, which could cause my son to be placed in the custody of the Department of Children and

Families. The violence that has occurred at the home is not something I want my son exposed to, nor am I willing to stand by and allow her to put him in a position to become a victim of it by being there. And why should he be subjected to sleeping on a couch with her, when he has his own bed in my home? I also want you to relay that she needs to start contributing to his welfare, by giving me at least forty to fifty dollars per week, and I will incur all the other expenses."

The mediator's position is supposed to be a neutral one while trying to encourage a resolution between the two parties. After showing the documents to support my claims about the home Audrey resided in, reiterating the late hours she worked, emphasizing I was granted a restraining order on the basis of the home being a dangerous place for my son, as well as the court petition to legally get custody based on all of the above, the mediator stated she understood my position.

Ms. Johnson added, "It may be in your son's best interest to stand firm in your reasons for not wanting him to be at her temporary house."

With that said, I became adamant. I was no longer willing to negotiate with Audrey if she insisted on my son being at the place she was living.

Ms. Johnson left again to speak with Audrey. This time, she stayed even longer. When she returned, she said, "Mr. Mack, I think we have reached an impasse. Ms. Beck is insistent that she be allowed to take her son to the home she lives in, and she now wants him to be able to stay overnight with her on her two days off, which are Sundays and Wednesdays. Furthermore, she stated she was not going to give you a dime for his support. Instead, she will buy things for him as needed."

I said, "He's three, so he doesn't need things like diapers or milk. What could she be talking about when she says she'll get what he needs?"

She replied, "Although I understand you, my objective is to remain neutral."

"Please, will you try one last time to convince her it would be in our son's best interest not to be at that home? I want her to look at it from that point, rather than like it's about her and me. Remind her that the court will take the same position of what's in the best interest of our son."

Ms. Johnson said, "I will give it a try."

Not more than two minutes passed before she returned this time, and said, "Ms. Beck accused me of being partial and rude to her. So I'm terminating the process."

I asked, "What happens next?"

"Your case will proceed to a hearing in front of a judge for care and custody to be addressed. But, as far as mediation, it will be reported that an agreement could not be reached."

"What if we had come to an agreement? What would have happened?"

"You both would have signed the documents stating the terms we agreed to. From there, we would still have had to go before a judge to legally finalize our agreement. But, you could have gone on with the task of raising your son together, although separate, without any further involvement from the court. Because we did not, a judge will now decide the outcome of every aspect of your son's life. That includes care, custody, primary residence, and even financial responsibilities. You will be informed of the court date within a few days. It normally takes a few weeks, but because of the circumstances of your case and a restraining order is involved, it will be heard by a judge sooner."

"Will you be sending a report to the judge about what took place during negotiations between my son's mother and me?"

"Yes, and I will get with my supervisor to let her know I was accused of being biased by the mother. With that, your case should be heard even sooner."

JOINT Custody

CHAPTER 4

The Court's Perspective

The bottom line when children are involved in family court, the standard will what's in the best interest of the child. The first time I was in front of a judge in family court, Audrey and I were told she was not going to play referee between us. Also, the judge made it clear she was aware of the problems between us, including the restraining order and what had taken place in mediation. I welcomed the judge's authority and stern admonition. I thought it would force Audrey to justify wanting to expose our son to the home she was residing in. This happened while she explained to the judge why she wanted to have our son sleep on a couch with her when I lived around the corner, where he had his own bed. She also had to explain why she felt like she did not have to contribute to his welfare since I was his temporary primary custodian.

So the rules were set, or so I thought. The judge turned her attention to each of us, but I was first. She asked, "What brought you to the point of petitioning the court for custody of your son?"

I began by saying, "Your Honor, I do everything for our son, while she works all night and sleeps all day." I went on to explain, "I cook for him at least five days a week. I wash all of his clothing; all of which I purchased. I dress and groom him for school every morning and bathe him every night. After school, I take him outside to play, ride in his car, go for a walk, or something that involves being outside. On the weekends, we'll go swimming, to a park, or somewhere like Chuck E. Cheese's. I also take him to all of his pediatrician appointments, making sure all his shots are up-to-date. Most importantly; I make sure he lives in a safe and comfortable home that's full of love and care."

Then I turned my focus to why I felt it was necessary for me to petition the court. I explained my main reason was because when Audrey would leave, she always wanted to drag Shiloh with her. By law, I knew there was nothing I could do or say to prevent this until I established paternity. I felt I needed to be acknowledged as his father by the courts to have rights to his care and custody. I expressed my concern about the house Audrey was living in and wanted him to visit her at. I proceeded to provide the court with all the copies of the police reports generated to and from the home. I shared how Audrey had started drinking heavily, taking pills, smoking pot, and even engaging in the use of cocaine which is what led to the demise of our relationship. The fact that she started using drugs caused her to become more and more detached from our personal life, and her involvement with our son became nonexistent. I owned the home we lived in before our separation, and I allowed her to live with me while she saved her money to get her own place.

After six months, she had not even accumulated $500, due to her increasing drug usage. I informed Audrey I would give her a few more months to save enough for her deposit and first month's rent. After this set time, I wanted her to leave. I told the judge Audrey worked in the adult entertainment industry and chose that over our family. I said this because I had been asking her to quit and get a regular job since the birth of our son, but she refused to stop it. Throughout this time, she would be high on drugs or impaired from alcohol. When my son saw her in this state, he always asked me what was wrong with her. To cover for her, I told him she did not feel well. I felt like she was using me for a place to sleep all day and do whatever she wanted to do all night. She was not contributing to any household expenses, or toward his needs.

The judge turned to Audrey and asked, "What's your response to these allegations he just made?"

From the moment she opened her mouth, nothing but lies about abuse came out. Audrey never responded to anything I said that caused me to petition the court for custody of our son, which is what the judge wanted to hear. She said, "He was emotionally and physically abusive to me."

The judge asked Audrey, "Do you have anything, such as police reports or hospital records to support your claims?"

She stated, "No."

Even without that, she was still allowed to say whatever she wanted, regardless of how outlandish it sounded. For instance, she claimed I abused her by waking her up after she had been working all night, to spend time with our son after I picked him up from school. Another example she gave was that I would ask her to bathe our son and read him a bedtime story. Audrey called this abuse because, as she told the judge, I knew she had to get ready for work, and the time I wanted her to bathe him was when she started to get ready for work. Audrey went on to say, "He was involved with other women I worked with, and he caused me to have to work in a hostile environment based on that. One day, he shoved me, causing me to fall after we engaged in a heated argument about me moving out."

I tried to make a statement to deny what she was saying, only to be told, "Please, remain silent," by the judge.

Hearing that was empowering to Audrey. At the time, I was getting upset, but then I remembered the judge's admonition about not playing the role of a referee between us. So I maintained my composure as she made more and more unfounded allegations against me.

I noticed, at times, Audrey said different things and the judge glanced at me to see what my response was. But, I looked her dead in the eyes each time and did not flinch. I didn't show any reaction.

The whole time Audrey was giving her testimony, she had to be told to refrain from using profanity in the courtroom.

In the beginning, I felt like I was being treated unfairly by the judge by not being allowed to respond to the things she was accusing me of. But then I thought, *Let her keep talking because the more she does, the worse she sounds.*

I'm sure the judge was thinking that if she was acting this way in front of her, Audrey was probably ten times worse outside of a courtroom. Almost everyone has sense enough to be respectful in a court of law.

By the time she was finished, I felt like I did not need to say anything in addition to what I had already said.

The judge made only a temporary ruling, but it was legal and binding. My son was to be left in my custody until further review. Audrey would be allowed to pick Shiloh up any time on Saturday mornings and return him no later than 8:00 p.m. On Sundays, she would be allowed to pick him up after 1:00 p.m., when church was over and she was to return him no later than 8:00 p.m. She could take him to the home she lived in, but was at no time to leave him unsupervised by her. She was not to use any drugs or alcohol while she had him. And if there were any parties or large gatherings at the home, she was not allowed to have him in that type of atmosphere.

Furthermore, Audrey was to submit to random drug screens from the court as our case proceeded, which would be conducted as we attended future court dates. The judge stated, "Miss, if you're using, you had better make sure you're clean before our next court date." If she tested positive for any drugs not prescribed by a physician, she would be required to only have supervised contact with our son.

The judge said, "Sir, you have to go to child support enforcement if you wish to have her contribute to his care and expenses. You can use the temporary court order to show that you're his primary custodian right now."

The judge continued, "The last issue I want to address is the restraining order." She ordered that we do all exchanges of our son in a public place and advised both of us not to violate any of the terms or conditions of the restraining order.

When Audrey called to say she wanted to pick our son up, I was to have him there on time at the designated place we agreed to meet. And she was to do the same when returning him.

Audrey tried to interrupt the judge, but the judge stated, "I've taken all the testimony I'm going to take at this time. I've made my rulings and expect both of you to abide by them."

The judge also ordered us back to mediation before returning to her courtroom, to see if we could reach an agreement outside of her rulings, or if we would leave them the way she ordered. She told Audrey she expected her to consider the order just put in place before starting negotiations.

But, Audrey never showed up for the second mediation; my next move was to research the different types of custody I could pursue.

CHAPTER 5

Joint Custody

There are three main types of custody that can be given by a court to either parent, whether they are the petitioner or the respondent.

I titled this book *Joint Custody,* because after my experience with family court, I came to the conclusion the courts are right in their belief that it is in a child's best interest for both parents to be involved in their lives. Therefore, joint custody is the best resolution for this to happen.

Joint custody can be agreed to by the parties, or ordered by a judge. As I stated in Chapter 3, mediation is mandatory for all cases involving children, whether it's from a couple having care and custody established by a court or one seeking a dissolution of a marriage. As I also stated before, even if joint custody is agreed on through mediation, it still has to be finalized by a judge.

Joint custody means the child can reside equally with both parents; both parents will have input as to education, healthcare, and social activities. The terms most agreed to or ordered by the court when joint custody is the outcome, is that the child/children will live with one parent for the school year and the other parent for the summer. The holidays are usually split, which includes birthdays, Mother's Day, Father's Day, Christmas, Thanksgiving, and New Year's Day. The issue of child support can be elevated with joint custody, if both parties agree to be responsible for the children's needs and expenses, while they are with the parent who has them. Or, one parent can still be ordered to pay, even with joint custody.

From my personal experience and through observation of others, including celebrities, a parent can be absent from a child's life for an entire childhood, and someone can tell the child every negative thing one can think of about the person, but as soon as the child gets old enough to look for the missing parent, he/she will.

The child will catch buses, planes, trains and even walk to find the parent. I'm not sure if it is inherent or instinctive, but no matter how good of a life a child is given, the child wants to know about his/her heritage.

From my experience as a child and father, I've felt both sides of this story. As a child, I was raised thinking one man was my father, when in fact, he and my mother married while she was pregnant with me. My biological father no longer wanted to be involved with my mother after she told him she was pregnant. So, when my mother got married, her husband legally adopted me. For the first thirteen years of my life, I thought he was my father when, in truth, he was not.

My Mom felt she needed to tell me the truth after my biological father wanted to be a part of my life. I can recall the first time I saw him. My Mom asked me to take her best friend, who lived next door, some coffee. That was nothing unusual, but what was unusual was that she wanted me to get dressed up to do it. After getting changed, I went over to Ms. Annie's house to give her the coffee. I planned to just hand it to her and leave. But she opened the door, and said, "Come on in; I want you to meet my friend."

I stepped inside, and this man was sitting there in the kitchen, smiling from ear to ear. He extended his hand to shake mine, and said, "I've been looking forward to meeting you for a long time."

My response was, "Why? Do you know me?"

"No, but I want to get to know you."

My next question was, "Do you know my dad?"

"Yes, and he's a good man for taking care of you."

We went back and forth with small talk for a few minutes. Then I asked Ms. Annie, "Can I go now?"

She said, "Yes."

When I got home, Mom was waiting for me at the door crying. I asked, "What's wrong?"

She said, "I'm fine. Did you meet a man over there?"

I replied, "Yes."

"What did you two talk about? Was he nice? Did you like him?"

After answering all of her questions, I asked, "How do you know him? Does my dad know him?"

She took me by the hand, led me to the couch, sat me down, and said, "The man you met wants to be like a big brother to you and take you places and be a part of your life."

My first questions were, "What will Dad say? Is he going to take my brother, too?"

My brother, Man, was two years older than me. At the time, we were inseparable. She said, "No, he just wants to take you first, and then he will start letting your brother come. Your dad is okay with him taking you out for fun, and he knows the man."

Later, I found out the man I knew as my dad felt betrayed by my mother for letting this man walk into my life, after he had taken care of me for thirteen years and considered me to be his son. He raised my brother and sisters with my Mom and me, but I was his special child. Because of this, he did not want to be involved with me meeting my biological father. But he knew this was the right thing to do whether he liked it or not.

The next week, I was picked up by the man I would come to know as Willie. We went to a restaurant to eat lunch. He took me by a few of his friend's houses to meet them, and they all said the same thing, "Man, you spit that one out," or "You can't deny that one."

One way or another, they all said I looked just like him. The next place we went to was his mother's house. The first thing she said when she saw me was, "That's my grandbaby!"

We ate there, and she asked me a hundred and one questions. This went on for what seemed like hours; she ended it by saying, "I want you to call me Grandma."

I said, "Yes, ma'am."

Mr. Willie was ready to go, so we said goodbye. She made me promise I would come back to see her.

Finally, Mr. Willie took me home. When I stepped through the door, Mom grabbed me and asked, "Are you all right? Was he nice to you? Where did you go? Who did you meet? Did you like him?"

I answered all of her questions; then I looked square into her eyes, and asked, "Mom, why was everybody saying I looked like Mr. Willie?"

She just hugged me and broke down crying. I managed to pry myself from her firm embrace and point blank asked, "Is Mr. Willie my real dad?"

Her only response was, "Baby, I'm sorry."

She said it over and over. I remember I just took off running. The more she screamed for me to come back, the faster I ran. I had no idea where I was running to or why. I just ran. I was sitting at the park crying; I looked up and saw my brother, whom my mother sent out to find me, coming toward me. Man came up to me but did not say a word. He just hugged me. Then he said, "Mom wanted me to come find you."

He took my hand, and I followed him without resistance. Once back home, Mom tried her best to explain how everything came to be and why.

I continued to see Mr. Willie, which is what I continued to call him throughout my life and until the end of his. And Louis, the man I thought was my father, I continued to call him Dad. I grew to love Mr. Willie, despite him not being in my life for the first thirteen years. In fact, the older I grew, the closer I got to him.

After Audrey and I separated, I still tried to leave a door open for her to be in Shiloh's life. I never talked bad about her to him, and I tried to keep him excited about seeing her. I did this regardless if she got involved with him or not.

As a parent, I think we should always leave a door open for the children to know the other parents. We should leave a door open and let the children close it on their own. If one parent closes the door on the child, he/she will open it and search for the other parent and even resent the one parent for trying to stop it.

The child won't care if someone says the mother or father is no good, a drunk, or a junkie, and never gave a dime toward child support. The child won't stop wanting to see the other parent because to him or her, it won't be about money. It will be about knowing who the other person is, what the person looks like, and above all to know if that person loves the child or not.

We hear this all the time, even from some of the biggest names in sports and entertainment, when someone is meeting one parent for the first time. After meeting, some of these relationships blossom into strong bonds, and some don't want to be involved any further.

It's good to keep this in mind when dealing with family court; it's in the best interest of the child to know both parents. This is the standard the court will base their final decision on. It all comes down to what's in the best interest of the child. It won't matter if one parent is rich or poor or if one parent is more educated than the other or what their race is or whose house is the nicest or who's bank account is bigger. The bottom line is none of that will outweigh what's in the child's best interest.

With this, I suggest when pursuing custody, start with joint custody to give the court the impression you have the child's best interest in mind. Regardless of whether you start out seeking joint custody or not, you can always go after primary or sole custody later. But, if you try from the beginning, it can give the court the impression you don't have the child's best interest in mind.

CHAPTER 6

Primary Custody

---◈---

Primary custody is probably the most common form of custody agreed to and awarded by the court. I would attribute this mainly to a lot of fathers being satisfied with the children staying with their mothers the majority of the time. Or when the court decides it would be in the best interest of the children to reside with their mothers.

Primary custody is when a child's home is established with one parent. The parent with primary custody is usually responsible for ensuring the child is in school, resolving health issues, social activities, and even discipline. Visitation may also be determined by the primary custodian for the other party, or it may be determined by the court if the two parties cannot agree.

My advice to any parent consenting to primary custody being granted to the other party is first to consider the things it could trigger such as child support, insurance coverage, and limited visitation.

I agree the non-custodian parent should be required to pay child support and the amount ordered can be drastic between joint and primary custody. The decision-making process could be affected dramatically, including input concerning the child.

When pursuing or consenting to the various types of custody, one needs to consider the long-term ramifications of the outcome. A parent could consent to primary custody now; but several years later, the parent could want joint custody or to become the primary custodian, and in extreme cases, even want to pursue sole custody.

So, imagine if your lifestyle changes or you're interested in being with your child more, but you have agreed to the other parent having primary custody. You will have to go back in front of a judge and relive the process of having a judge decide all those issues again. The reason I said this is because, in all likelihood, when a parent has had primary custody for say five years, then the other parent decides he/she now wants to have the child's living arrangements split 50/50, more often than not, the primary parent is not going to agree with that. It may be because the parent may not like the other's new spouse, or think the other parent is doing it for the purpose of not having to pay child support, or other various reasons.

I know of some cases where one parent has primary custody, but the child spends time equally with both parents, and the non-custodian still pays child support. This could be because of the very things I just stated. As time passes, and the emotions calm down, some parents become more civil to each other and follow the court's lead on what's in the best interest of the child.

When decisions are finalized in courts; that order will remain legal and binding until the child becomes eighteen years old, unless the child goes to college. Then child support can be enforced until the age of twenty or graduation, whichever comes first. Although child support is still enforced until the child turns twenty-one, once the child turns eighteen, he/she is considered an adult and can choose which parent to reside with.

Once I learned the different types of custody, I pursued primary custody for both of my sons, Shiloh and Adonis. I was the petitioner in one case and in the other, I was the respondent. When I first filed the case, I opened it seeking joint custody. But, once the cases were presented to judge, I pursued primary custody.

I've heard a lot of guys say they want to be a part of their children's lives because their fathers were not a part of their lives, and they know how it made them feel.

To me, it goes deeper than that. I have never been able to understand how a man can look at his own child, know it's his child, the child is the spitting image of him, and he does not want to be involved with the child. The thought of having to pay child support, in his mind, should not be legal. Some men, if they deserve to be called that, have gone to the extreme of killing their child's mother, just to avoid paying child support. Some people try to pretend they are exempt from a court order to pay child support, which will lead to it being deducted from checks, income tax returns being seized, and even being arrested.

I pursued custody of my other son, Shiloh, because his mother was involved in the adult entertainment industry, which became more than her job; it became her lifestyle.

Because of either parent's occupation or even lack thereof, the outcome and type of custody granted is not determined by that. But, in my case, Audrey let her job interfere with her responsibilities as a mother. I used that and her drug use to my advantage to get custody. Although my sons had different mothers, I did not look at their mothers being different; I looked at both of my sons as being the same—both mine.

Honestly, I did not expect to get primary custody of one of my sons and sole custody of the other one. My intent was to be recognized legally as their father and have legal rights to them, so I would not have to deal with their mothers on their terms.

When all was said and done, the court made its decision based on the best interest of my sons and did not base it on who could put the other parent down the most.

Even when I was given primary custody of Shiloh, I still left the door open to his mother to visit him whenever she wanted. Whenever she lost focus, I helped her regain it by reminding her of the court's order stating she was granted limited visitation, and at my discretion, she could see him more.

I had to make sure I went by the court's orders, as well as she did. The reason the court got involved was because we, the parents, could not come to an agreement. If I went outside of that order to let her see our son more and it led to a conflict between us, it would make me look like I was irresponsible because the court order is put in place to prevent conflicts. Once the case is closed, the parent given primary custody must consider the risk of having that changed by the court because the parent did not abide by the orders.

Judges are firm about their rulings. By the time a case reaches them, and they make a final decision, the parties will have failed to come to terms through mediation or multiple court hearings leading up to a judge giving a ruling. So, when the judge rules in your favor, it's best to tell the other party that if he/she wants it to have it modified, he/she will need to go back and petition the court to have a hearing set to have it done.

So many custody cases end up being a lengthy, time consuming, contentious process. The person ending up with primary or sole custody will not be willing to compromise after the case is finalized, especially if the other party has made disparaging remarks or false accusations.

Even if one parent files for primary custody and the other party is not seeking primary custody. I still suggest the parent contest it and ask that joint custody be granted to both parties. A court could look at someone not contesting primary custody by the other party as a sign that the one parent is not looking to be involved in the child's life full-time.

The bottom line is if you have joint custody, you always have equal rights to your child, even if you don't exercise those rights. If you decide to do so at a later time, those rights will be in place. But, again, if the court grants primary custody to one parent, it will be up to that parent to be willing to grant more time to the other without returning to court and re-opening the case.

Here's a prime example of a man who did not contest his son's mother pursuing primary custody. When their case was finalized, his son was five years old. He and the child's mother had gotten married. The father was allowed weekend visits with his son every other weekend. The mother's husband treated the child as if he was his son and had negative feelings for his father because he did not want to be in his son's life full-time. He felt like he was more of a father than his actual father, because of the things he'd taught him to do, like taking him to play sports and raising him as a father should. The child turned twelve and then, his biological father saw his son was his spitting image and knew to be with him now, would not be like it was when he was five. The boy can now take his own baths, feed himself, get dressed on his own, do his homework, and all the little things the father would have done for him when he was five. So the father wants to have the child over more, and his wife also embraces the child. But the mother's husband feels like he's done the hard part of raising him and now his father wants to show up to be his dad. His anger causes his wife to be reluctant to let the child spend more time with his birth father because she does not want her husband to feel like he's being betrayed by her or her son. The husband is insistent that she abides by the final court order and not expand visits with his father because it could re-open the door for problems.

The biological father feels he has been a father to his son because he's been paying child support the whole time. Although he did not pick him up every other weekend the way he had a right to do, his son knew who he was, and they had a loving relationship.

When the father realized the mother was not willing to let his son spend more time with him, they started accusing each other all over again and included each other's spouses. The mother used the son's father's new wife as a reason why she did not want their son to spend more time with him; the father stated the same about the mother's new husband as the reason the child needed to be with him more.

Now, the son was caught in the middle of their dispute. On one hand, he loved his stepfather and did not want him to feel like he was betraying him, as his mother also felt.

But he loved his father and wanted to spend more time with him. In his mind, if he did not say that, his father would think he would rather be with his stepdad more than with him.

This puts a twelve-year-old kid in a bad position, trying to please both sets of parents. The father would not have had this problem if he had sought joint custody instead of going along with the mother being granted primary custody. The only resolution to this case is to go back to court to have the custody status modified.

While the court may side with the father in granting more visitation, the custody status may stay the same regarding the mother being the primary custodian. The real problem will be that it could take months to go back through mediation and get before a judge again to have the original order modified. Above that, it will take a toll on the child, which is not in the best interest of the child. And keep in mind, this is the standard by which all family courts base their decisions.

JOINT Custody

CHAPTER 7

Sole Custody

S ole custody means the party it's granted to will have absolute care and control of the child; the other party may or may not have limited visitation. In most cases, when sole custody was awarded, the other party appeared to be a serious problem to the court, to the extent of refusing to follow the court orders, one party posed a threat to the other party or, in extreme cases, one party was verbally, mentally, emotionally, or physically abusive to the child.

While sole custody is granted the least often, it can still be pursued when a parent initially petitions the court or the respondent can do so when responding.

When sole custody is sought by a parent, it's usually a mother doing so because she, and maybe the child, has been abused by the father. She will say they are living in fear of the father and in most of these cases; she will have an order of protection against him.

Sole custody can also be granted through consent. This happens when one parent decides not to have anything to do with the child and is willing to give up parental rights by not contesting custody.

The fair part about all the types of custody is that they are all reversible. A person consenting to sole custody can later petition the court for joint custody or even sole custody. An example is a mother who was granted sole custody by the court or through consent. She was involved in a relationship where the child was abused in some fashion. The child was placed in the care of the Department of Children and Families. The first thing they try to do is place the child in the care of a relative.

Their first option will always be with the other parent, but if that parent has given up parental rights, the child won't be placed there. The parent can petition the court to have sole custody of the child. As long as a parent's parental rights have not been terminated by a court, the parent will always have some rights to the child, even when the other party has sole custody.

Only a judge can legally terminate a parent's parental rights.

Here's an example to show when sole custody is given to one party that the other parent still has some rights. Imagine a mother having sole custody. She and the child get involved in a car accident. The mother passes, and the child is in critical condition, requiring surgery that could save the child's life or cause it to end. Consent is needed to do the procedures. The next person able to give that consent is the other parent.

Regardless of what type of custody the mother had, it still does not terminate the father's rights. In some cases, one parent can be given sole custody, and the other parent can be ordered not to have any contact with the child. But that will be a temporary order. A judge cannot specifically order that a parent not have contact for life with the child, this would be equivalent to terminating one's parental rights. Let me clarify, judges can order whatever they want, but it still has to be consistent with the law. So, even if a judge gives one parent sole custody and orders the other parent to have no contact, the parent still will have some rights left intact.

Another misconception about a parent consenting to the other parent having sole custody is that it will stop them from having to pay child support. That's not true; if it were, millions of men, and some women, would be asking the courts to give the custodian sole custody of the child, so they would not have to pay support.

Regardless if one parent does not want to be involved in the child's life, it does not negate the fact that the child still needs to be supported by both parents, even if it's just financially by one of them.

My case with Karen, Adonis' mother, became so contentious it spanned two counties, multiple restraining orders, arrests, and culminated with him ultimately being kidnapped by her.

The state and county of a child's birth are where custody must be pursued. A child can't be born in Florida, be moved to New York by one parent, and the other parent tries to go to New York seeking custody.

My son, Adonis, was born in Tampa, Florida, in Hillsborough County. His mother tried to go to Orlando to petition the court for custody. Orlando is where she was originally from and where her parents still lived. She was told that she had to petition the court in the county where our son was born. By the time she tried to petition in Tampa, I already had. We were ordered into mediation when the case was opened; we agreed our son would be exchanged weekly and we were responsible for his expenses while he was in our care and custody.

This went smoothly for a while, as we awaited our case to be presented to a judge. Throughout this time, Karen was strongly trying to convince me to reconcile our differences and resume our relationship. At first, I was open to the suggestion, thinking we would not have to deal with having to go to court for months; we could get back together, never go back to court, and the case would be closed. Family court is a branch of civil court, which means it's not a crime if you don't show up for civil court hearings.

I decided not to go along with her suggestion after realizing she was not interested in reuniting for the benefit of our son. She wanted to do it to have control over me. In her mind, she figured I would think she'd done me a favor if she dropped the case and this would make me want to be with her again. Every little thing that came up between us, she would always threaten to proceed with the custody case. From that, I decided it would be in my best interest to go forward with the case and seek primary custody.

The reason I wanted primary custody was because Karen had moved several times, indicating she did not have stable housing. She was unemployed and living with her parents and a few of her siblings; she did not have her own room, and neither did our son. Also, she was involved in an automobile accident, rendering her disabled. More importantly, I felt I would be showing the court I wanted custody as much as she did by requesting primary custody. Even if I did fall short of that, the next thing would be joint custody. That's all I really wanted anyway. But I felt I needed to counter her petition for primary custody by seeking the same relief.

The agreement we came to was no longer being honored by her. When it came time to pick up our son, Karen would go to Orlando on the day of the exchange and tell me to drive the other fifty miles to get him. The exchange was supposed to occur in Tampa, where we both lived. On more than one occasion, I drove to Orlando to pick up my son, only to be told his mother had taken him to Tampa to drop him off to me.

Karen's father, John, got involved and threatened to kill me to the point the court issued a restraining order, banning him from being present at any of the exchanges for our son because when he was present, he made threats. I recorded him several times and presented multiple voice messages he'd left on my voicemail to the court.

Despite being ordered to stay away from me and have no contact, John repeatedly violated the injunction of protection, which led to his arrest.

On a day I was supposed to pick my son up, I asked for the exchange to happen in a public place, and Karen agreed. Upon reaching the agreed upon place, I decided to call the sheriff's office and asked him to be present at the exchange. I did not want to be accused of any wrongdoings. I told the receptionist about the restraining order I had, and I feared it would be violated without an officer being present. By the time the officer arrived, Karen, John, and my son were pulling up to the McDonald's. They did not recognize me because I was in another truck, not my own. Karen called my cell phone and said if I was not there in five minutes, she was leaving. I said, "I'm inside waiting for you."

They did not see the sheriff's car because it was on the other side of the building. But I was in a position where the sheriff could see me sitting at a table, and he could see them as they entered the restaurant. John was the first one through the door. I got up, walked outside to the sheriff's vehicle, and informed him that was the person the restraining order was against. The sheriff approached John and asked his name. When the sheriff verified who he was and that he knew I had a restraining order against him and had been served a copy, John was placed under arrest. I got my son and left.

This put even more tension between Karen and me. This is because she felt like I set her father up to be arrested. She kept trying to say I knew he would not harm me in any way. I said, "Tell him to convince the judge who granted the one-year restraining order against him that he was not serious."

When all was said and done, I was granted primary custody of my son. This came after what's called a social investigation. A social investigation can be ordered by the court or requested by either the petitioner or the respondent.

Once the social investigation was done and he recommended I be given primary custody, Karen left the state with our son and had to be tracked down by the Florida Department of Law Enforcement, better known as the FDLE. She was told that if she did not return our son to me, she would be charged with interfering with child custody and possibly kidnapping. By the time they located her, she was in Pittsburgh, Pennsylvania, living on a reservation. Since she was Native American, Karen thought she could shield our son from state laws by hiding out there. However, officers informed her that she only had twenty-four hours to release Adonis to them or her case would be reported to the Federal Bureau of Investigations for their assistance. After hearing that,

Karen agreed to release our son to the local police department, and Child Protective Services took custody of Adonis from there.

Meanwhile, I was in an emergency court hearing set by Mr. Escobar that same day, giving me an order from the same judge who had presided over our hearing. I was to pick up my son from Pennsylvania the next day. The court's order claimed jurisdiction and ordered that my son be turned over to me and be returned to Tampa, Florida. She also set a hearing for the day after I returned with my son. The Center for Missing and Exploited Children paid for my round-trip ticket to fly to Pittsburgh to get my son.

As I look back, I can recall a gentleman from the Department of Children and Families in Pittsburg locking eyes with me when I raised my hand to let him know who I was. I knew he was the right man because he was holding my son. As he approached me, it was apparent he was saying something to my son because Adonis turned, and when he saw me, he lit up like a Christmas tree. He stretched out his arms for me saying, "Daddy! Daddy! Where you been?"

Fighting back the tears, I replied, "Looking for you, son."

The feeling I had is beyond words. It's a feeling that can only be felt by a parent who truly loves his/her child. Recalling this scene, makes me hurt all over again.

I showed the gentleman the court order proving that Adonis was to be given to me only and returned to Florida. I also showed him my driver's license to verify who I was.

If it wasn't for the social investigation, I don't know if the outcome would have been the same.

I flew back to Florida the same day I got my son. The next morning, I was in family court where I was given a temporary order granting me sole custody of my son. His mother was ordered to have supervised visits at the Children's Justice Center for one year before the order would even be considered for modification. The Children's Justice Center is basically a part of the courthouse. Parents who have been ordered visits there are on camera, and the visit is for one hour, once a week.

A social investigation will expose things in your family you may not even be aware of. Some could be beneficial, and some could be detrimental.

CHAPTER 8

Social Investigation

---◆---

A social investigation is when an officer from the court goes to the petitioner and the respondent's home. A thorough and extensive background check is done on both parties, including their family members. This means background checks will be done on brothers, sisters, mother, father, and may include grandparents.

The investigator will speak to neighbors and school officials to see which parent was involved in the child's schooling and other activities. They will speak to the child's physician to see which party has been involved in assuring the child's medical needs are being met. They will check finances to see if the parties are financially secure. Above all, they will try to discern which party has the child's best interest in mind.

The parent with the child's best interest in mind will be willing to encourage a relationship with the other parent, as well as follow the agreements between the parties, and the orders given by the court.

In the case involving my son, Shiloh, a social investigation was ordered by the court because looking back on it, the judge could not make a ruling on which of us had our son's best interest in mind based on her acting out of spite, and me responding out of malice.

The custody case involving my son, Shiloh, was contentious, to say the least, and ended up in dependency court. But, as far as reaching the point of being extreme, the matter involving Adonis went beyond extreme.

As I mentioned in the last chapter, Adonis' grandfather got involved to the extent that a restraining order was issued against him. He violated it and was subsequently arrested for doing so.

Once the social investigation was ordered, the senior investigator was assigned our case. He scheduled a time and date to meet me at my home to do an evaluation.

When he arrived that day, I was prepared for what I thought would be an interview. Instead, it ended up being more like an interrogation. He asked if I finished high school, the name of the school, what year I graduated. He went on to ask if I had been in the military, or had I ever been arrested, when, for what, where and the disposition of it. Did I use drugs or alcohol? Would I submit to a drug and alcohol screen? How long had I been living at the current house? Did I rent or own the home? How much I paid for the monthly mortgage, insurance, property taxes? What was the name of the finance company? Was I a member of any banks? Did I have a savings or checking account or both? Was my truck leased, owned, or was I still making payments? How much were the payments and insurance? How much were my average utility and water bills? How much did I spend on groceries each month? What were my monthly expenses for my son for school supplies, projects, trips, clothing, snacks, etc.? He asked who took my son to his last doctor's visit. What was the doctor's name, phone number, address and if there was an e-mail address?. When was the last time I spoke to any school official? Where my son attended school? Who were his specific teachers? What were their classroom numbers?

Then he turned and started asking questions about my mother and father. Did they marry? If so, did they divorce? How old was I when they divorced? Who did I live with after the divorce? Did I visit with the other parent regularly or was it joint custody? Did I live with both parents equally? Had either parent been to prison, college, or the military? Were my parents alive or deceased? When I told him both were deceased, he asked what caused their deaths. How old they were when they passed? How many brothers and sisters I had? I replied, "I have one brother and three sisters."

He stated, "Let's start with your brother."

It was basically the same questions about all them. Had they been in the military, prison, or college? Were they married? Did they have children? Where did they live? Did I have frequent contact with them? Were they employed and where?

The next thing he wanted to do was look around my home. He started in the kitchen. When I say he started in the kitchen, I mean, he actually wanted to see inside the drawers where I kept spoons, forks, etc. Then he looked inside the cabinets where I kept pots and pans. He checked inside the refrigerator, freezer, the pantry, and made sure the oven and stove worked.

My washer and dryer were set up in an area off from the kitchen. At his request, I turned them on to show they both worked. We went to my son's room, where I opened the drawers to show his clothes, underwear, and socks. I opened the closet with his shoes and showed the clothes hanging on hangers. I took him to my linen closet, so he could see I had additional sheets for my son, as well as towels, washcloths, and extra hygiene products.

I showed him my restroom; I turned on the shower, flushed the toilet, and turned on the faucet to prove everything was in working order. The last place was my room, which he just briefly looked in.

Then he asked to see where I kept the toys, books, and school supplies. I led him to the closet in my guest room, which I had made into a playroom. He could see there were enough toys there for several kids.

After all this, I thought, *What else could he possibly want to know.* That's when he asked could we take a seat again so he could ask me a couple more questions before he left. The first was how do I discipline my son? I explained my son was a good kid and did not need discipline with more than, "Stop that," or "Don't do that; that's enough of that." The only time I would actually spank his hands was if he and his brother fought each other. I used time-outs and sent them to bed early if they got into any other things I considered trouble. The last question was, "Are you on any type of medication for any kind of mental illness?"

I declared, "No!"

I assumed he would write a report and render his decision from there. But he spoke with my neighbors, my son's teachers, my brother, and sisters, and did a background check on me to see if I had ever been arrested.

A social investigation is an extensive, thorough process. If one is ordered, you have to be prepared to have your life reviewed from all angles. All the questions I faced should be assumed as routine for everyone. Everything is investigated from the living room to the bedroom, to the kitchen, and the backyard.

Although they are called investigators, they should be looked at as interrogators and the eyes and ears for the judge deciding your custody case. The judge will regard the investigator's report as if they had done the investigation themselves. Ninety-nine percent of the time if not 100 percent, the judge will base a decision on the investigator's recommendations.

If a petitioner or respondent feels the court is leaning toward giving custody to the other parent, they can request to the judge that a social investigation be done, or the judge may order it in cases when there are a lot of conflicts between the parties. However, evidence must show that both parties have genuine interests in the custody of the child. But either can be considered by the court to come closer to the court's standard than the other party, which is who has the child's best interest in mind.

Regardless of which type of custody a parent pursues, I feel if they keep in mind what the court will use to base their decision on, which is what's in the best interest of the child, the party who does will find favor from the court.

All in all, if you get involved in a child custody case and hear the words *social investigation*, bring your A game and play to win, or you will lose!

JOINT Custody

CHAPTER 9

Dependency Court

◆

Dependency court is for extreme cases in which children are removed from one or both of the parents. Most often, the child will be taken by Child Protective Services for reasons that could range from abuse of the child to a presumed risk of danger to the child, exposure to violence between parents, neglect, and drug use or exposure to drugs or in some cases, unsanitary living conditions.

When a child is removed from a parent, a court date will be set for the parent to appear in front of a dependency court judge within twenty-four hours. Besides the judge, the person who removed the child from the parent will be present at the hearing. In some cases, the supervisor who authorized the removal will also be present. In Tampa, Florida, there will be someone from The Department Children and Families. This is an agency that is subcontracted by Child Protective Services to find and maintain housing and supervision for the child once removed from the home. There will be a guardian ad litem representative, which is someone who maintains contact with the child to ensure safety and needs are being met. They are independent of the other agencies and serve as an extra set of eyes and ears for the court. Also, someone from the Attorney General's Office will be present. When a child is removed from parents, the child is considered to be in the custody of the state they are in.

In the hearing, the reasons the children were removed will be stated to the judge, and the assistant attorney will, more than likely, side with those reasons. If the judge determines there is sufficient probable cause to warrant the removal, the child will remain in the care and custody of the state and under the jurisdiction of the court.

It is a custom of the court to try to find a direct family member to place the child with. This process will involve a criminal background check as well as a drug screen. The potential relative will have an evaluation of their home to ensure it's up to standards and the relative will be able to provide a safe and adequate home for the child. When this process is over, and the home is approved, the child will be placed with the relative and monitored by the different agencies. The home will be subjected to random visits by these different agencies and possibly continue to make sure the child is either attending daycare or school, staying up-to-date with all medical appointments, and attending the scheduled court hearings.

In the event no family member steps up, the child will be placed in a foster home or group home. The parent or parents will then be given what's called a *case plan*. A case plan is basically the things the agencies and the judge set as requirements that have to be met before the child can be returned to the parent. This could consist of drug screens, parenting classes, anger management courses, stable housing, and employment. The minimum time this will go on is six months. If all the conditions are met by the parent, the case can be closed.

This would mean the parent will no longer be supervised and all of the parental rights will be restored. The faster the parent complies, the sooner the child will be returned. But, even if the parent meets all the requirements, the case will remain open for a minimum of six months. This means if the child was with a relative for six months, and the parent has the child returned, the parent will still have the case opened with the court for an additional six months. Every time a child is placed in a different home, the timeline starts over for the six months of visits to the home, court hearings, and the child is still being considered under the guidance of the state.

If the child is in the care of a relative or the state, and the parent is not in compliance with the court's order or their case plan, the case will continue to remain open and proceed in the direction of the child becoming a ward of the state. The relative the child is placed with can be given long-term guardianship. The child can also be placed for adoption if both parents' parental rights are terminated.

If the child is returned to a parent after meeting all the court orders, and the child gets removed again, the process will start all over again. Matter of fact, the child can be removed several times from a parent and be returned as long as they complete their case plan.

Even in dependency court, the standards are the same as with all branches of family court, meaning what's in the best interest of the child.

When a child is taken, the parent has the right to request a hearing be held that will be like a bench trial where the judge will weigh the facts and allegations and decide whether they're true or if they lack sufficient evidence to substantiate the reasons for which the child was removed. If the party is deemed to be guilty, it will automatically open a case for six months. This is regardless if the child is returned or placed with a relative or even foster care. The judge can find a parent guilty, withhold adjudication, and return the child to the parent with a case plan and supervision by various agencies. The judge can find the parent guilty and order the child not be returned until the case plan is complete or at least in compliance by the parent. Last and least often, the judge could conclude the reasons the child was removed were not proven by the state and return the child to the parent.

The reason I included dependency court in this book is to bring attention to how extreme some cases can become with everyone involved in a custody matter. Dependency court should be considered by parents when they become hostile to each other. It should be considered when a child is being abused, not to mention the parent being arrested. It should be considered when a child is being neglected or when a parent's drug use or the child's exposure to drugs could result in the child being removed.

Most importantly, a parent should consider the devastating effect it could have on the child to be removed from the home and placed with strangers.

One would think that when a child is removed, someone in the family would step in and try to have the child placed with them to prevent placement in foster care. But there are hundreds of thousands of children in foster care. Some will spend their entire childhood being moved from home to home. Some are placed there from birth until they become eighteen. Some can be placed in foster care with a brother or sister and get separated for life.

Dependency court is for extreme cases, and the consequences can be extreme. It will ruin a parent and child for the rest of their lives. The moral of the story is: don't say you want what's best for your child, and then you become the reason he/she is placed in dependency court. There's a saying that goes, "You can do something in a few minutes that can take months or years to get out of."

Regardless of how a parent may feel about the child's other parent pursuing custody, keep in mind that if both parents act reckless, the child can be removed from them. Remember the court will always, always rule in favor of what's in the best interest of the child! No exceptions!

CHAPTER 10

The Cost of Lawyers

———————⬧———————

W hen pursuing custody of a child or children through family court, hiring the right attorney could make the difference in the outcome of your case. Keep in mind, first and foremost, it's business to them. While winning cases is a priority for them, getting paid for doing so is of even more significance.

In most cases, the attorneys opposing parties hire are familiar with each other from past cases, where they were counsels for individuals in either divorce cases, divorce cases involving children, or in child custody matters. It seems the higher the stakes are, the more contentious the attorneys become toward each other. This is because the more assets and finances there are, the more the attorney stands to receive when the case is settled.

I've seen cases where the two parties could and would have resolved the case, but their attorneys were so focused on each other and who would be considered the winner between them until the case went on much longer than was necessary. Dragging a case on benefits the attorney also because he/she will be charging for all the hours spent litigating. This will be for work done in and outside the courtroom pertaining to your case. This could include phone calls, office visits, time spent on the internet, etc.

When this particular case was over, I was left wondering if the conflicts between the attorneys were staged. In the courtroom, they were not only attacking each other's clients, but they were also attacking each other to the point where the judge had to keep admonishing them for their courtroom etiquette and threatened both with contempt of court.

The reason I say it appeared to be staged was because both of them insisted on the case being continued, which meant more charges for their clients. But here's what really caught my attention: when the case was finally resolved, the two attorneys who had been threatened with contempt of court met in the hallway, shook hands and hugged while smiling, laughing, and complimenting one another on being a great opponent.

In some cases, the judge can and will order that one party has to pay the other's attorney's fees as part of the settlement. In my case, we were both ordered to pay our own attorney fees. Both attorneys probably felt they won regardless of what the outcome was for their clients. Consider this, when parties hire attorneys, they are representing you, they are speaking for you. So when they are in court telling a judge how terrible the other parent is, a judge will view this as something you're saying. Remember judges know the procedures of family court. They know, first, you and the other parent could not resolve the issues and come to an agreement, which led to a case being opened. Secondly, you and the other parent could not compromise in mediation.

In knowing this, keep in mind the courts perspective is what's in the best interest of the child. If your attorney is in court in front of a judge requesting sole custody without anything to justify it; it won't fly. Again, seek joint custody, so the judge will see that you are putting the child's best interest first before any bad feelings you may have between you and the other parent.

If you hire an attorney, and you see him/her getting personal with the other attorney, talk to them and let them know you want to resolve the case as soon as possible, which means savings for you. But also that you want the judge to know you're willing to work with the other parent for the benefit of the child.

The bottom line is when your case is over, the attorneys will probably be in court the next day with different clients, and six months later, you will have to remind them who you are. That is, unless they received a substantial payment as part of your case being resolved.

The best thing to do is to try to come to an agreement with the other parent about the care and custody of the child. This will keep you and your child out of the court system for at least eighteen years.

If the problem is personal between you and the other parent, all of that needs to be put aside for the sake of the child.

Both parents need to be mature enough so it won't take a county judge to tell you how to raise your child, where, and when each parent can see the child and how much to contribute to your child's welfare.

Although it may seem like I've thrown attorneys under the bus in this chapter, there are some good lawyers in family court doing great jobs and have their client's interests in mind. The great ones will be easy to identify because they will tell you from the start what's in the best interest of the child will be the standard that has to be met.

When considering the hiring of an attorney, do so as a last resort. I hope this book will serve as a guide to avoid the whole family court process.

To any woman considering custody or support, try to work with the child's father to resolve these matters. Don't take him to court out of malice because he's moved on and entered a new relationship. In doing this, weigh the fact that you will be subjecting you and your child to the same system. As I've discussed in this book, it could lead to the extreme, which is dependency court. Give the father the benefit of the doubt and let him know you want or need him to contribute to the welfare of the child without the courts getting involved. Even let him read this book, so he will be informed of the process of the family court, and know he has a choice to be in his child's life. Once a case is opened, his choice can become something that's forced, at least the finance part. This way, you will have a clean conscience that you did all you could to keep your child from being in the court *system* because of you.

To any man involved in a custody matter, if the child is yours, you should not need a judge to tell you to contribute to the child's welfare. Either way, you will end up doing it, by choice or by force. Child support can be worse than parole if you don't comply. As I stated in a previous chapter, failing to pay can result in numerous things happening. Income tax returns forfeited, liens placed on property, driver's license suspended, funds taken directly out of checks, warrants being placed for your arrest, and your credit rating will be affected because child support shows up on your credit report.

Regardless of how you may feel toward the child's mother, keep in mind the court will not be concerned with that. And, if anything, the more negative things you have to say is more reason for you, as a parent, to want to be in the child's life to protect the child from all that negativity.

Try to come to terms with helping out financially for the child, even if you chose not to be otherwise involved with the child.

If it gets to the point of court, and you are the respondent, respond! If you don't, you will lose by default! The payments could be lower, and visitation with your child can be established without the mother being able to interfere such as the mother telling you the child cannot be around your new spouse or how long and when you can visit.

I addressed the women readers, as well as the men. But those statements can be interchangeable. What I said to the mothers, can be for the fathers, and what I said to the fathers, can be for the mothers.

The moral of this chapter, work it out without lawyers or the courts. Once you're in the system, you and your kids will be there even when the case is closed for at least eighteen years.

Find the same level of respect you had for each other when you made the child and respect each other as parents.

If you can't, I know a lawyer who will be more than happy to help you!

JOINT Custody

Summary

Family court should only be used as a last resort. Every reasonable effort should be put forth by both parents to avoid subjecting you and your child to a system that can last until the child becomes eighteen. An agreement can be reached when the child is merely one-year-old, and the case considered closed. However, the order that will be given will last and be enforceable until the child turns eighteen.

Every child deserves to know both of their parents. If neither parent poses a risk of danger to the child, then every court in America will allow them to be a part of the child's life.

In some cases, it will be necessary for the courts to intervene. In these cases, the courts can greatly benefit a parent. If all has been done to avoid conflicts, and they still occur, a parent should not hesitate on getting into family court.

Four ways that will certainly open a case in family court is through:

1. A dissolution of a marriage and a child is involved.

2. Through simply petitioning the court to open a case.

3. When a restraining order is filed, and a child is included.

4. A child is placed in dependency court.

I can tell you from my personal experience, family court can be both beneficial and intrusive. If I had it to do all over again, more than likely I would, because the circumstances surrounding my case were extremely contentious between my sons' mothers and me. When the courts got involved, all the problems were resolved.

Consider that when children see adults arguing, especially their parents, it can have a devastating effect on them. Consider that children will naturally love both parents. So to speak negatively, be mentally, or physically abusive in front of them, will impact them. More than anything consider what's in their best interest.

It's best to put all differences aside and try to come up with solutions both parties can agree to, even if it takes getting a mutual family member or friend to mediate. If a couple is separating and the kids are old enough, involve them in the arrangements being agreed upon. If the kids see the parents getting along, and know both parents will be in their lives, it could make the transition easier for them.

In closing, respect each other and remember the other parent is just that, your child's other parent!

Love your children, put them first, and above all let the bottom line always be what's in the best interest of your child.

JOINT Custody

ACKNOWLEDGMENTS

Mrs. Sheila Mack, my brother's keeper, thank you for believing in me and for being vigilant toward the Mack brothers. In knowing the boys were safe with you, I was able to focus on writing this book. Your love, guidance, and nurturing spirit toward them were truly virtuous. Please, continue to love them, and I will raise them to always love you. We're all we've got.

JOINT Custody

About the Author

I've often been told I have three last names, Randolph Warren Mack. I feel blessed to say that I have lived 52 years of life's experiences and look forward to a lifetime more. Currently, I reside in the Florida, "The Sunshine State".

I have 3 wonderful sons; Shiloh 17, Adonis 16 and Giavonnie 10. My lovely wife, Michelle was extremely instrumental in helping me get this book published. I was inspired to write by my cousin, Alphonso Pinkney who wrote several books while being a sociologist and long-term chairman of the Department Of Sociology at Hunter College in New York.

As a youth while visiting my grandmother's home every Sunday after church for Sunday dinner, my brother, sisters and I were basically restricted to what was called "the T.V. room" where our options were to read a book or sit and watch wrestling with my grandfather. I would always pick up one of Alphonso's books and was fascinated by his writings.

As I got older I got back into reading which eventually led me to start writing. By the time I realized it I had written 5 books, a series of children's books and over 50 poems.

I give you my assurance that by purchasing my book you will find it to be a great guide and tool when dealing with the family court system.

www.ingramcontent.com/pod-product-compliance
Lightning Source LLC
Chambersburg PA
CBHW060630210326
41520CB00010B/1545